THE HIGH-PROTEIN OVERNIGHT OATS RECIPES

40+ Delicious Mouthwatering Oats For Healthy Morning Made From Nutritious Ingredients

AMADA L. HEATH

Copyright © 2024 by Amada L. Heath

All rights reserved. No part of this book may be reproduced in any form or by any electronic or mechanical means, including information storage and retrieval systems, without permission in writing from the publisher, except by a reviewer, who may quote brief passages in a review.

TABLE OF CONTENT

INTRODUCTION
CHAPTER 1: HIGH-PROTEIN OVERNIGHT OATS
CHAPTER 2: BENEFITS OF OVERNIGHT OATS
CHAPTER 3: HEALTHY RECIPES
    Protein-Packed Peanut Butter Banana Overnight Oats
    Berry Bliss High-Protein Overnight Oats
    Tropical Paradise Protein Overnight Oats
    Chocolate Banana Protein Overnight Oats
    Apple Cinnamon Protein Overnight Oats
    Savory Tomato and Basil Protein Overnight Oats
    Green Goddess Spinach and Avocado Protein Overnight Oats
    Mocha Hazelnut High-Protein Overnight Oats
    Spiced Pumpkin Pie Protein Overnight Oats
    Mediterranean Chickpea and Feta Protein Overnight Oats
    Almond Joy Protein Overnight Oats
    Vanilla Blueberry Protein Overnight Oats
    Pecan Maple Pumpkin Protein Overnight Oats
    Mango Coconut Chia Protein Overnight Oats
    Raspberry Dark Chocolate Protein Overnight Oats
    Caprese Inspired Tomato Basil Protein Overnight Oats
    Cinnamon Roll Protein Overnight Oats
    Black Forest Chocolate Cherry Protein

Overnight Oats
Maple Walnut Banana Protein Overnight Oats
Spinach and Sundried Tomato Protein Overnight Oats
Orange Creamsicle Protein Overnight Oats
Mexican Chocolate Protein Overnight Oats
Protein-Packed Espresso Overnight Oats
Lemon Poppy Seed Protein Overnight Oats
Mocha Almond Crunch Protein Overnight Oats
Cranberry Orange Protein Overnight Oats
Raspberry Almond Protein Overnight Oats
Apple Walnut Spice Protein Overnight Oats
Green Apple Pistachio Protein Overnight Oats
Tropical Mango Macadamia Protein Overnight Oats
Blueberry Cheesecake Protein Overnight Oats
Hazelnut Banana Bread Protein Overnight Oats
Pineapple Coconut Protein Overnight Oats
Matcha Green Tea Protein Overnight Oats
Raspberry Coconut Almond Protein Overnight Oats
Carrot Cake Protein Overnight Oats
Mango Raspberry Protein Overnight Oats
Banana Nut Bread Protein Overnight Oats
Chocolate Mint Protein Overnight Oats
Maple Pecan Protein Overnight Oats
Strawberry Banana Protein Overnight Oats
Caramel Apple Protein Overnight Oats
Peanut Butter & Jelly Protein Overnight Oats

Spiced Apricot Almond Protein Overnight Oats
CONCLUSION

BONUS: WEEKLY MEAL PLANNER JOURNAL

INTRODUCTION

My mornings used to be a blur of fumbled alarms, rushed breakfasts, and a grumbling stomach by mid-morning. That all changed when I discovered the power of high-protein overnight oats.

Now, my mornings are a symphony of calm efficiency. The night before, I whip up a jar of oats in just minutes. It's a simple ritual - a scoop of rolled oats, a swirl of plant-based milk, a dollop of Greek yogurt, a sprinkle of chia seeds, and a burst of flavor with some berries or cocoa powder. I mix it all together, screw on the lid, and leave it in the fridge overnight.

The magic happens while I sleep. The oats soften and absorb the flavors, the chia seeds plump up, and the yogurt adds a creamy richness. In the morning, I wake up to a breakfast that's ready and waiting, no cooking required.

The difference is remarkable. The protein in the oats and yogurt keeps me feeling full and satisfied for hours, unlike the sugary cereals or toast that used to leave me reaching for snacks by 10 am. I have more energy, I focus better, and I'm no longer plagued by that dreaded mid-morning slump.

It's not just about convenience; it's about setting the tone for a healthy day. Starting my morning with a nutritious and satisfying meal allows me to make better choices throughout the day. I'm less likely to grab unhealthy snacks when I'm feeling hangry, and I have more energy to hit the gym or go for a walk.

Overnight oats have become a game-changer for my mornings. They're a delicious, easy, and protein-packed way to start my day off right, one healthy and satisfying bite at a time.

CHAPTER 1: HIGH-PROTEIN OVERNIGHT OATS

Overnight oats, a staple in many health-conscious diets, have gained popularity for their simplicity, convenience, and adaptability. The concept revolves around soaking raw oats in liquid – typically milk or a dairy-free alternative – and allowing them to sit in the refrigerator overnight. This no-cook method results in a creamy and delicious breakfast that can be customized to suit individual tastes and nutritional goals.

When it comes to high-protein overnight oats, the focus shifts to incorporating ingredients that elevate the protein content of the meal. Proteins are essential for various bodily functions, including muscle repair, immune system support, and maintaining satiety. By infusing overnight oats with protein-rich elements, this breakfast option becomes a powerhouse of nutrients.

Key protein boosters in high-protein overnight oats recipes include Greek yogurt, a dairy product renowned for its high protein concentration and creamy texture. Mixing in protein powder is another popular strategy, providing an additional protein punch without altering the oats' texture significantly. Nuts and seeds, such as chia seeds, hemp seeds, or almonds, contribute not only to protein content but also to the overall texture and nutritional profile.

The high-protein overnight oats recipes often feature a thoughtful combination of ingredients. Rolled oats provide complex carbohydrates and fiber, ensuring a sustained release of energy throughout the morning. The liquid component, whether milk or a plant-based alternative, not only serves as a medium for soaking but also introduces more protein to the mix.

CHAPTER 1: HIGH-PROTEIN OVERNIGHT OATS

Overnight oats, a staple in many health-conscious diets, have gained popularity for their simplicity, convenience, and adaptability. The concept revolves around soaking raw oats in liquid – typically milk or a dairy-free alternative – and allowing them to sit in the refrigerator overnight. This no-cook method results in a creamy and delicious breakfast that can be customized to suit individual tastes and nutritional goals.

When it comes to high-protein overnight oats, the focus shifts to incorporating ingredients that elevate the protein content of the meal. Proteins are essential for various bodily functions, including muscle repair, immune system support, and maintaining satiety. By infusing overnight oats with protein-rich elements, this breakfast option becomes a powerhouse of nutrients.

Key protein boosters in high-protein overnight oats recipes include Greek yogurt, a dairy product renowned for its high protein concentration and creamy texture. Mixing in protein powder is another popular strategy, providing an additional protein punch without altering the oats' texture significantly. Nuts and seeds, such as chia seeds, hemp seeds, or almonds, contribute not only to protein content but also to the overall texture and nutritional profile.

The high-protein overnight oats recipes often feature a thoughtful combination of ingredients. Rolled oats provide complex carbohydrates and fiber, ensuring a sustained release of energy throughout the morning. The liquid component, whether milk or a plant-based alternative, not only serves as a medium for soaking but also introduces more protein to the mix.

Furthermore, flavor enhancers like fruits, spices, and natural sweeteners make these high-protein overnight oats a delicious and satisfying breakfast option. The versatility of the recipes allows individuals to experiment with different ingredients, tailoring the meal to their preferences while meeting their protein needs. Ultimately, the high-protein overnight oats approach combines the ease of preparation with the nutritional benefits of a protein-rich diet, making it a wholesome and practical choice for those seeking a balanced start to their day.

CHAPTER 2: BENEFITS OF OVERNIGHT OATS

High-protein overnight oats offer several benefits that make them a popular and nutritious choice for breakfast:

1. Muscle Support and Repair: Protein is crucial for muscle health, and incorporating high-protein ingredients like Greek yogurt, milk, and nuts into overnight oats provides essential amino acids necessary for muscle support and repair.

2. Satiety and Weight Management: Protein-rich meals tend to be more filling, promoting a sense of satiety and reducing the likelihood of overeating throughout the day. This can be particularly beneficial for those aiming to manage their weight.

3. Sustainable Energy: The combination of complex carbohydrates from oats and the sustained release of energy from protein creates a breakfast option that provides lasting energy throughout the morning, helping to avoid energy crashes.

4. Convenience: The "overnight" aspect of the oats means minimal morning preparation. Simply mix the ingredients the night before, refrigerate, and grab a ready-to-eat, nutritious breakfast in the morning – a time-saving solution for busy individuals.

5. Versatility: High-protein overnight oats recipes are highly customizable. Individuals can tailor the ingredients to their taste preferences and dietary needs, incorporating a variety of fruits, nuts, seeds, and flavorings.

6. Nutrient Density: In addition to protein, overnight oats can be enriched with a variety of nutrient-dense ingredients such as chia seeds, flaxseeds, and nuts, providing essential vitamins, minerals, and healthy fats.

7. Digestive Health: Oats are a good source of soluble fiber, which aids in digestion and promotes a healthy gut. Including fiber-rich ingredients like chia seeds further contributes to digestive well-being.

8. Blood Sugar Regulation: The combination of protein and fiber in high-protein overnight oats can help regulate blood sugar levels, providing a steady release of glucose into the bloodstream and preventing rapid spikes.

9. Adaptability to Dietary Preferences: Whether someone follows a vegetarian, vegan, or gluten-free diet, high-protein overnight oats can be adapted to meet various dietary preferences and restrictions, making them a versatile choice for a broad range of individuals.

10. Taste and Enjoyment: Beyond their nutritional benefits, high-protein overnight oats can be delicious. The addition of fruits, spices, and sweeteners ensures a satisfying and enjoyable breakfast experience.

7. Digestive Health: Oats are a good source of soluble fiber, which aids in digestion and promotes a healthy gut. Including fiber-rich ingredients like chia seeds further contributes to digestive well-being.

8. Blood Sugar Regulation: The combination of protein and fiber in high-protein overnight oats can help regulate blood sugar levels, providing a steady release of glucose into the bloodstream and preventing rapid spikes.

9. Adaptability to Dietary Preferences: Whether someone follows a vegetarian, vegan, or gluten-free diet, high-protein overnight oats can be adapted to meet various dietary preferences and restrictions, making them a versatile choice for a broad range of individuals.

10. Taste and Enjoyment: Beyond their nutritional benefits, high-protein overnight oats can be delicious. The addition of fruits, spices, and sweeteners ensures a satisfying and enjoyable breakfast experience.

CHAPTER 3: HEALTHY RECIPES

Protein-Packed Peanut Butter Banana Overnight Oats

Ingredients:
- Rolled oats (1/2 cup)
- Greek yogurt (1/2 cup)
- Milk (1/2 cup)
- Protein powder (1 scoop)
- Peanut butter (2 tbsp)
- Banana (1, sliced)
- Chia seeds (1 tbsp)
- Honey (1 tbsp, optional)

Instructions:
1. In a jar or container, combine rolled oats, Greek yogurt, milk, protein powder, and mix well.
2. Add sliced banana, peanut butter, chia seeds, and honey (if using).
3. Stir until all ingredients are evenly distributed.

4. Seal the container and refrigerate overnight.
5. In the morning, give it a good stir and enjoy!

Berry Bliss High-Protein Overnight Oats

Ingredients:
- Rolled oats (1/2 cup)
- Cottage cheese (1/2 cup)
- Almond milk (1/2 cup)
- Vanilla protein powder (1 scoop)
- Mixed berries (1/2 cup)
- Almonds (2 tbsp, chopped)
- Maple syrup (1 tbsp, optional)

Instructions:
1. Combine rolled oats, cottage cheese, almond milk, and protein powder in a jar.
2. Add mixed berries, chopped almonds, and maple syrup if desired.
3. Mix well and refrigerate overnight.

4. Give it a gentle stir in the morning and savor the berry goodness!

Tropical Paradise Protein Overnight Oats

Ingredients:
- Rolled oats (1/2 cup)
- Coconut milk (1/2 cup)
- Greek yogurt (1/4 cup)
- Pineapple (1/2 cup, diced)
- Mango (1/2 cup, diced)
- Shredded coconut (2 tbsp)
- Protein powder (1 scoop)
- Almond butter (1 tbsp)

Instructions:
1. In a jar, combine rolled oats, coconut milk, Greek yogurt, and protein powder.
2. Add diced pineapple, mango, shredded coconut, and almond butter.
3. Mix thoroughly and refrigerate overnight.
4. Wake up to a tropical delight!

Chocolate Banana Protein Overnight Oats

Ingredients:
- Rolled oats (1/2 cup)
- Milk (1/2 cup)
- Greek yogurt (1/4 cup)
- Chocolate protein powder (1 scoop)
- Banana (1, mashed)
- Cocoa powder (1 tbsp)
- Almond butter (1 tbsp)
- Dark chocolate chips (1 tbsp)

Instructions:
1. Combine rolled oats, milk, Greek yogurt, and chocolate protein powder in a jar.
2. Add mashed banana, cocoa powder, almond butter, and dark chocolate chips.
3. Mix well and refrigerate overnight.
4. Top with additional banana slices and chocolate chips before serving.

Apple Cinnamon Protein Overnight Oats

Ingredients:
- Rolled oats (1/2 cup)
- Apple (1, grated)
- Almond milk (1/2 cup)
- Vanilla protein powder (1 scoop)
- Greek yogurt (1/4 cup)
- Cinnamon (1/2 tsp)
- Walnuts (2 tbsp, chopped)
- Maple syrup (1 tbsp, optional)

Instructions:
1. In a jar, combine rolled oats, grated apple, almond milk, protein powder, and Greek yogurt.
2. Add cinnamon, chopped walnuts, and maple syrup if desired.
3. Mix thoroughly and refrigerate overnight.
4. Enjoy the comforting flavors of apple and cinnamon in the morning!

Savory Tomato and Basil Protein Overnight Oats

Ingredients:
- Rolled oats (1/2 cup)
- Cottage cheese (1/2 cup)
- Tomato (1, diced)
- Basil (2 tbsp, chopped)
- Parmesan cheese (2 tbsp, grated)
- Sun-dried tomatoes (1 tbsp, chopped)
- Salt and pepper to taste
- Olive oil (1 tbsp)

Instructions:
1. In a jar, combine rolled oats, cottage cheese, diced tomato, chopped basil, and grated Parmesan.
2. Add sun-dried tomatoes, salt, pepper, and olive oil.
3. Mix well and refrigerate overnight.
4. Wake up to a savory and protein-packed breakfast!

Green Goddess Spinach and Avocado Protein Overnight Oats

Ingredients:
- Rolled oats (1/2 cup)
- Greek yogurt (1/2 cup)
- Almond milk (1/4 cup)
- Spinach (1 cup, chopped)
- Avocado (1/2, mashed)
- Chia seeds (1 tbsp)
- Lemon juice (1 tbsp)
- Salt and pepper to taste

Instructions:
1. Combine rolled oats, Greek yogurt, almond milk, chopped spinach, and mashed avocado in a jar.
2. Add chia seeds, lemon juice, salt, and pepper.
3. Mix thoroughly and refrigerate overnight.
4. Enjoy a green and nutritious start to your day!

Mocha Hazelnut High-Protein Overnight Oats

Ingredients:
- Rolled oats (1/2 cup)
- Coffee (1/4 cup, cooled)
- Chocolate protein powder (1 scoop)
- Hazelnut butter (2 tbsp)
- Almond milk (1/4 cup)
- Chopped hazelnuts (1 tbsp)
- Dark chocolate shavings (1 tbsp, optional)
- Maple syrup (1 tbsp, optional)

Instructions:
1. In a jar, combine rolled oats, cooled coffee, chocolate protein powder, and hazelnut butter.
2. Add almond milk, chopped hazelnuts, and dark chocolate shavings if desired.
3. Mix well and refrigerate overnight.
4. Wake up to a mocha-flavored delight!

Spiced Pumpkin Pie Protein Overnight Oats

Ingredients:
- Rolled oats (1/2 cup)
- Pumpkin puree (1/4 cup)
- Vanilla protein powder (1 scoop)
- Almond milk (1/4 cup)
- Pumpkin spice blend (1 tsp)
- Pecans (2 tbsp, chopped)
- Maple syrup (1 tbsp, optional)

Instructions:
1. Combine rolled oats, pumpkin puree, vanilla protein powder, and almond milk in a jar.
2. Add pumpkin spice blend, chopped pecans, and maple syrup if desired.
3. Mix thoroughly and refrigerate overnight.
4. Enjoy the flavors of fall in a nutritious breakfast!

Mediterranean Chickpea and Feta Protein Overnight Oats

Ingredients:
- Rolled oats (1/2 cup)
- Greek yogurt (1/4 cup)
- Milk (1/4 cup)
- Chickpeas (1/4 cup, cooked)
- Feta cheese (2 tbsp, crumbled)
- Cherry tomatoes (1/2 cup, halved)
- Cucumber (1/4 cup, diced)
- Kalamata olives (1 tbsp, sliced)
- Fresh parsley (2 tbsp, chopped)
- Olive oil (1 tbsp)
- Lemon juice (1 tbsp)
- Salt and pepper to taste

Instructions:
1. In a jar, combine rolled oats, Greek yogurt, milk, cooked chickpeas, and crumbled feta.
2. Add halved cherry tomatoes, diced cucumber, sliced Kalamata olives, and fresh parsley.
3. Drizzle with olive oil, lemon juice, salt, and pepper.

4. Mix well, ensuring the ingredients are evenly distributed.
5. Refrigerate the jar overnight.
6. In the morning, give the mixture a good stir.
7. Top with extra fresh parsley and a drizzle of olive oil if desired.
8. Enjoy a Mediterranean-inspired, protein-packed breakfast!

Almond Joy Protein Overnight Oats

Ingredients:
- Rolled oats (1/2 cup)
- Almond milk (1/2 cup)
- Greek yogurt (1/4 cup)
- Chocolate protein powder (1 scoop)
- Almonds (2 tbsp, chopped)
- Coconut flakes (2 tbsp)
- Dark chocolate chips (1 tbsp)
- Almond butter (1 tbsp)
- Maple syrup (1 tbsp, optional)

Instructions:
1. Combine rolled oats, almond milk, Greek yogurt, and chocolate protein powder in a jar.
2. Add chopped almonds, coconut flakes, dark chocolate chips, almond butter, and maple syrup if desired.
3. Mix well and refrigerate overnight.
4. Wake up to the deliciousness of an Almond Joy-inspired breakfast!

Vanilla Blueberry Protein Overnight Oats

Ingredients:
- Rolled oats (1/2 cup)
- Vanilla protein powder (1 scoop)
- Almond milk (1/2 cup)
- Greek yogurt (1/4 cup)
- Blueberries (1/2 cup)
- Vanilla extract (1/2 tsp)
- Almond butter (1 tbsp)
- Chia seeds (1 tbsp)
- Honey (1 tbsp, optional)

Instructions:
1. In a jar, combine rolled oats, vanilla protein powder, almond milk, and Greek yogurt.
2. Add blueberries, vanilla extract, almond butter, chia seeds, and honey if desired.
3. Mix thoroughly and refrigerate overnight.
4. Enjoy the sweet and creamy goodness of vanilla and blueberries in the morning!

Pecan Maple Pumpkin Protein Overnight Oats

Ingredients:
- Rolled oats (1/2 cup)
- Pumpkin puree (1/4 cup)
- Vanilla protein powder (1 scoop)
- Almond milk (1/4 cup)
- Pecans (2 tbsp, chopped)
- Maple syrup (1 tbsp)
- Pumpkin spice blend (1 tsp)
- Greek yogurt (1/4 cup)
- Cinnamon (1/2 tsp)

Instructions:
1. Combine rolled oats, pumpkin puree, vanilla protein powder, almond milk, and Greek yogurt in a jar.
2. Add chopped pecans, maple syrup, pumpkin spice blend, and cinnamon.
3. Mix well and refrigerate overnight.
4. Wake up to the delightful flavors of pecan, maple, and pumpkin spice!

Mango Coconut Chia Protein Overnight Oats

Ingredients:
- Rolled oats (1/2 cup)
- Coconut milk (1/2 cup)
- Greek yogurt (1/4 cup)
- Mango (1/2 cup, diced)
- Vanilla protein powder (1 scoop)
- Shredded coconut (2 tbsp)
- Chia seeds (1 tbsp)
- Honey (1 tbsp, optional)

Instructions:
1. In a jar, combine rolled oats, coconut milk, Greek yogurt, and vanilla protein powder.
2. Add diced mango, shredded coconut, chia seeds, and honey if desired.
3. Mix thoroughly and refrigerate overnight.
4. Enjoy the tropical fusion of mango and coconut in the morning!

Raspberry Dark Chocolate Protein Overnight Oats

Ingredients:
- Rolled oats (1/2 cup)
- Almond milk (1/2 cup)
- Greek yogurt (1/4 cup)
- Chocolate protein powder (1 scoop)
- Raspberries (1/2 cup)
- Dark chocolate chips (1 tbsp)
- Almond butter (1 tbsp)
- Chia seeds (1 tbsp)
- Maple syrup (1 tbsp, optional)

Instructions:
1. Combine rolled oats, almond milk, Greek yogurt, and chocolate protein powder in a jar.
2. Add raspberries, dark chocolate chips, almond butter, chia seeds, and maple syrup if desired.
3. Mix well and refrigerate overnight.
4. Indulge in the rich flavors of raspberry and dark chocolate in the morning!

Caprese Inspired Tomato Basil Protein Overnight Oats

Ingredients:
- Rolled oats (1/2 cup)
- Greek yogurt (1/4 cup)
- Milk (1/4 cup)
- Cherry tomatoes (1/2 cup, halved)
- Mozzarella cheese (2 tbsp, diced)
- Fresh basil (2 tbsp, chopped)
- Balsamic glaze (1 tbsp)
- Olive oil (1 tbsp)
- Salt and pepper to taste

Instructions:
1. In a jar, combine rolled oats, Greek yogurt, milk, halved cherry tomatoes, and diced mozzarella.
2. Add chopped fresh basil, balsamic glaze, olive oil, salt, and pepper.
3. Mix thoroughly and refrigerate overnight.
4. Wake up to a savory and protein-packed Caprese-inspired breakfast!

Cinnamon Roll Protein Overnight Oats

Ingredients:
- Rolled oats (1/2 cup)
- Almond milk (1/2 cup)
- Vanilla protein powder (1 scoop)
- Greek yogurt (1/4 cup)
- Cinnamon (1 tsp)
- Pecans (2 tbsp, chopped)
- Cream cheese (1 tbsp)
- Maple syrup (1 tbsp, optional)

Instructions:
1. Combine rolled oats, almond milk, vanilla protein powder, and Greek yogurt in a jar.
2. Add cinnamon, chopped pecans, cream cheese, and maple syrup if desired.
3. Mix well and refrigerate overnight.
4. Experience the comforting taste of a cinnamon roll in your breakfast oats!

Black Forest Chocolate Cherry Protein Overnight Oats

Ingredients:
- Rolled oats (1/2 cup)
- Chocolate protein powder (1 scoop)
- Almond milk (1/2 cup)
- Greek yogurt (1/4 cup)
- Cherries (1/2 cup, pitted and halved)
- Dark chocolate chips (1 tbsp)
- Almond butter (1 tbsp)
- Chia seeds (1 tbsp)
- Honey (1 tbsp, optional)

Instructions:
1. In a jar, combine rolled oats, chocolate protein powder, almond milk, and Greek yogurt.
2. Add pitted and halved cherries, dark chocolate chips, almond butter, chia seeds, and honey if desired.
3. Mix thoroughly and refrigerate overnight.
4. Wake up to the delightful blend of chocolate and cherries in your oats!

Maple Walnut Banana Protein Overnight Oats

Ingredients:
- Rolled oats (1/2 cup)
- Almond milk (1/2 cup)
- Banana (1, mashed)
- Vanilla protein powder (1 scoop)
- Greek yogurt (1/4 cup)
- Maple syrup (1 tbsp)
- Walnuts (2 tbsp, chopped)
- Cinnamon (1/2 tsp)
- Almond butter (1 tbsp)

Instructions:
1. Combine rolled oats, almond milk, mashed banana, vanilla protein powder, and Greek yogurt in a jar.
2. Add maple syrup, chopped walnuts, cinnamon, and almond butter.
3. Mix well and refrigerate overnight.
4. Enjoy the comforting flavors of maple and walnuts in your morning oats!

Spinach and Sundried Tomato Protein Overnight Oats

Ingredients:
- Rolled oats (1/2 cup)
- Greek yogurt (1/4 cup)
- Milk (1/4 cup)
- Sundried tomatoes (2 tbsp, chopped)
- Spinach (1 cup, chopped)
- Feta cheese (2 tbsp, crumbled)
- Olive oil (1 tbsp)
- Lemon juice (1 tbsp)
- Salt and pepper to taste

Instructions:
1. In a jar, combine rolled oats, Greek yogurt, and milk.
2. Add chopped sundried tomatoes, chopped spinach, crumbled feta, olive oil, lemon juice, salt, and pepper.
3. Mix thoroughly and refrigerate overnight.
4. Wake up to a savory, Mediterranean-inspired breakfast with the goodness of spinach and sundried tomatoes!

Orange Creamsicle Protein Overnight Oats

Ingredients:
- Rolled oats (1/2 cup)
- Vanilla protein powder (1 scoop)
- Orange juice (1/4 cup)
- Greek yogurt (1/4 cup)
- Orange zest (1 tsp)
- Almond slices (2 tbsp)
- Honey (1 tbsp, optional)

Instructions:
1. Combine rolled oats, vanilla protein powder, orange juice, and Greek yogurt in a jar.
2. Add orange zest, almond slices, and honey if desired.
3. Mix thoroughly and refrigerate overnight.
4. Wake up to the refreshing taste of an orange creamsicle-inspired breakfast!

Mexican Chocolate Protein Overnight Oats

Ingredients:
- Rolled oats (1/2 cup)
- Chocolate protein powder (1 scoop)
- Almond milk (1/2 cup)
- Greek yogurt (1/4 cup)
- Cinnamon (1/2 tsp)
- Chopped pecans (2 tbsp)
- Dark chocolate chips (1 tbsp)
- Vanilla extract (1/2 tsp)
- Maple syrup (1 tbsp, optional)

Instructions:
1. In a jar, combine rolled oats, chocolate protein powder, almond milk, and Greek yogurt.
2. Add cinnamon, chopped pecans, dark chocolate chips, vanilla extract, and maple syrup if desired.
3. Mix well and refrigerate overnight.
4. Savor the rich and spicy flavors of Mexican chocolate in your oats!

Protein-Packed Espresso Overnight Oats

Ingredients:
- Rolled oats (1/2 cup)
- Coffee (1/4 cup, cooled)
- Vanilla protein powder (1 scoop)
- Almond milk (1/4 cup)
- Almond butter (1 tbsp)
- Sliced bananas (1/2 cup)
- Cacao nibs (1 tbsp)
- Maple syrup (1 tbsp, optional)

Instructions:
1. Combine rolled oats, cooled coffee, vanilla protein powder, almond milk, and almond butter in a jar.
2. Add sliced bananas, cacao nibs, and maple syrup if desired.
3. Mix thoroughly and refrigerate overnight.
4. Wake up to the energizing flavors of espresso in your oats!

Lemon Poppy Seed Protein Overnight Oats

Ingredients:
- Rolled oats (1/2 cup)
- Greek yogurt (1/4 cup)
- Milk (1/4 cup)
- Lemon zest (1 tsp)
- Vanilla protein powder (1 scoop)
- Poppy seeds (1 tbsp)
- Blueberries (1/4 cup)
- Almonds (2 tbsp, sliced)
- Agave nectar (1 tbsp, optional)

Instructions:
1. In a jar, combine rolled oats, Greek yogurt, milk, lemon zest, and vanilla protein powder.
2. Add poppy seeds, blueberries, sliced almonds, and agave nectar if desired.
3. Mix thoroughly and refrigerate overnight.
4. Enjoy the bright and zesty combination of lemon and poppy seeds!

Mocha Almond Crunch Protein Overnight Oats

Ingredients:
- Rolled oats (1/2 cup)
- Coffee (1/4 cup, cooled)
- Chocolate protein powder (1 scoop)
- Almond milk (1/4 cup)
- Almond butter (1 tbsp)
- Sliced almonds (2 tbsp)
- Dark chocolate chips (1 tbsp)
- Vanilla extract (1/2 tsp)
- Maple syrup (1 tbsp, optional)

Instructions:
1. Combine rolled oats, cooled coffee, chocolate protein powder, almond milk, and almond butter in a jar.
2. Add sliced almonds, dark chocolate chips, vanilla extract, and maple syrup if desired.
3. Mix well and refrigerate overnight.
4. Wake up to the indulgent flavors of mocha and almond crunch in your oats!

Cranberry Orange Protein Overnight Oats

Ingredients:
- Rolled oats (1/2 cup)
- Vanilla protein powder (1 scoop)
- Orange juice (1/4 cup)
- Greek yogurt (1/4 cup)
- Dried cranberries (2 tbsp)
- Walnuts (2 tbsp, chopped)
- Orange zest (1 tsp)
- Honey (1 tbsp, optional)

Instructions:
1. In a jar, combine rolled oats, vanilla protein powder, orange juice, and Greek yogurt.
2. Add dried cranberries, chopped walnuts, orange zest, and honey if desired.
3. Mix thoroughly and refrigerate overnight.
4. Enjoy the festive combination of cranberry and orange in your morning oats!

Raspberry Almond Protein Overnight Oats

Ingredients:
- Rolled oats (1/2 cup)
- Almond milk (1/2 cup)
- Vanilla protein powder (1 scoop)
- Greek yogurt (1/4 cup)
- Raspberries (1/2 cup)
- Almond butter (1 tbsp)
- Slivered almonds (2 tbsp)
- Chia seeds (1 tbsp)
- Agave nectar (1 tbsp, optional)

Instructions:
1. Combine rolled oats, almond milk, vanilla protein powder, and Greek yogurt in a jar.
2. Add raspberries, almond butter, slivered almonds, chia seeds, and agave nectar if desired.
3. Mix well and refrigerate overnight.
4. Wake up to the delightful combination of raspberry and almond in your oats!

Apple Walnut Spice Protein Overnight Oats

Ingredients:
- Rolled oats (1/2 cup)
- Apple (1, grated)
- Almond milk (1/2 cup)
- Vanilla protein powder (1 scoop)
- Greek yogurt (1/4 cup)
- Walnuts (2 tbsp, chopped)
- Cinnamon (1/2 tsp)
- Nutmeg (1/4 tsp)
- Maple syrup (1 tbsp, optional)

Instructions:
1. In a jar, combine rolled oats, grated apple, almond milk, vanilla protein powder, and Greek yogurt.
2. Add chopped walnuts, cinnamon, nutmeg, and maple syrup if desired.
3. Mix thoroughly and refrigerate overnight.
4. Enjoy the warm and comforting flavors of apple, walnut, and spice!

Green Apple Pistachio Protein Overnight Oats

Ingredients:
- Rolled oats (1/2 cup)
- Almond milk (1/2 cup)
- Vanilla protein powder (1 scoop)
- Greek yogurt (1/4 cup)
- Green apple (1, diced)
- Pistachios (2 tbsp, chopped)
- Chia seeds (1 tbsp)
- Honey (1 tbsp, optional)

Instructions:
1. Combine rolled oats, almond milk, vanilla protein powder, and Greek yogurt in a jar.
2. Add diced green apple, chopped pistachios, chia seeds, and honey if desired.
3. Mix well and refrigerate overnight.
4. Wake up to the refreshing combination of green apple and pistachio in your oats!

Tropical Mango Macadamia Protein Overnight Oats

Ingredients:
- Rolled oats (1/2 cup)
- Coconut milk (1/2 cup)
- Mango (1/2 cup, diced)
- Vanilla protein powder (1 scoop)
- Greek yogurt (1/4 cup)
- Macadamia nuts (2 tbsp, chopped)
- Shredded coconut (2 tbsp)
- Chia seeds (1 tbsp)
- Honey (1 tbsp, optional)

Instructions:
1. In a jar, combine rolled oats, coconut milk, diced mango, vanilla protein powder, and Greek yogurt.
2. Add chopped macadamia nuts, shredded coconut, chia seeds, and honey if desired.
3. Mix thoroughly and refrigerate overnight.
4. Enjoy the tropical paradise of mango and macadamia in your morning oats!

Blueberry Cheesecake Protein Overnight Oats

Ingredients:
- Rolled oats (1/2 cup)
- Greek yogurt (1/4 cup)
- Almond milk (1/4 cup)
- Vanilla protein powder (1 scoop)
- Blueberries (1/2 cup)
- Cream cheese (2 tbsp, softened)
- Almond butter (1 tbsp)
- Chia seeds (1 tbsp)
- Maple syrup (1 tbsp, optional)

Instructions:
1. In a jar, combine rolled oats, Greek yogurt, almond milk, and vanilla protein powder.
2. Add blueberries, softened cream cheese, almond butter, chia seeds, and maple syrup if desired.
3. Mix well and refrigerate overnight.
4. Wake up to the delightful taste of blueberry cheesecake!

Hazelnut Banana Bread Protein Overnight Oats

Ingredients:
- Rolled oats (1/2 cup)
- Almond milk (1/2 cup)
- Vanilla protein powder (1 scoop)
- Banana (1, mashed)
- Hazelnuts (2 tbsp, chopped)
- Cinnamon (1/2 tsp)
- Nutmeg (1/4 tsp)
- Almond butter (1 tbsp)
- Maple syrup (1 tbsp, optional)

Instructions:
1. Combine rolled oats, almond milk, vanilla protein powder, and mashed banana in a jar.
2. Add chopped hazelnuts, cinnamon, nutmeg, almond butter, and maple syrup if desired.
3. Mix thoroughly and refrigerate overnight.
4. Enjoy the comforting aroma and taste of hazelnut banana bread!

Pineapple Coconut Protein Overnight Oats

Ingredients:
- Rolled oats (1/2 cup)
- Coconut milk (1/2 cup)
- Greek yogurt (1/4 cup)
- Vanilla protein powder (1 scoop)
- Pineapple (1/2 cup, diced)
- Shredded coconut (2 tbsp)
- Macadamia nuts (2 tbsp, chopped)
- Chia seeds (1 tbsp)
- Honey (1 tbsp, optional)

Instructions:
1. In a jar, combine rolled oats, coconut milk, Greek yogurt, and vanilla protein powder.
2. Add diced pineapple, shredded coconut, chopped macadamia nuts, chia seeds, and honey if desired.
3. Mix thoroughly and refrigerate overnight.
4. Wake up to the tropical goodness of pineapple and coconut!

Matcha Green Tea Protein Overnight Oats

Ingredients:
- Rolled oats (1/2 cup)
- Almond milk (1/2 cup)
- Vanilla protein powder (1 scoop)
- Greek yogurt (1/4 cup)
- Matcha green tea powder (1 tsp)
- Kiwi (1, sliced)
- Pistachios (2 tbsp, chopped)
- Honey (1 tbsp, optional)

Instructions:
1. Combine rolled oats, almond milk, vanilla protein powder, Greek yogurt, and matcha green tea powder in a jar.
2. Add sliced kiwi, chopped pistachios, and honey if desired.
3. Mix thoroughly and refrigerate overnight.
4. Start your day with the vibrant and antioxidant-rich flavors of matcha!

Raspberry Coconut Almond Protein Overnight Oats

Ingredients:
- Rolled oats (1/2 cup)
- Coconut milk (1/2 cup)
- Vanilla protein powder (1 scoop)
- Greek yogurt (1/4 cup)
- Raspberries (1/2 cup)
- Shredded coconut (2 tbsp)
- Almonds (2 tbsp, sliced)
- Chia seeds (1 tbsp)
- Agave nectar (1 tbsp, optional)

Instructions:
1. In a jar, combine rolled oats, coconut milk, vanilla protein powder, and Greek yogurt.
2. Add raspberries, shredded coconut, sliced almonds, chia seeds, and agave nectar if desired.
3. Mix thoroughly and refrigerate overnight.
4. Wake up to the delightful combination of raspberry, coconut, and almonds!

Carrot Cake Protein Overnight Oats

Ingredients:
- Rolled oats (1/2 cup)
- Almond milk (1/2 cup)
- Vanilla protein powder (1 scoop)
- Greek yogurt (1/4 cup)
- Carrot (1, grated)
- Walnuts (2 tbsp, chopped)
- Raisins (1 tbsp)
- Cinnamon (1/2 tsp)
- Maple syrup (1 tbsp, optional)

Instructions:
1. Combine rolled oats, almond milk, vanilla protein powder, Greek yogurt, and grated carrot in a jar.
2. Add chopped walnuts, raisins, cinnamon, and maple syrup if desired.
3. Mix thoroughly and refrigerate overnight.
4. Enjoy the delightful taste of carrot cake in your morning oats!

Mango Raspberry Protein Overnight Oats

Ingredients:
- Rolled oats (1/2 cup)
- Coconut milk (1/2 cup)
- Vanilla protein powder (1 scoop)
- Greek yogurt (1/4 cup)
- Mango (1/2 cup, diced)
- Raspberries (1/4 cup)
- Coconut flakes (2 tbsp)
- Chia seeds (1 tbsp)
- Agave nectar (1 tbsp, optional)

Instructions:
1. In a jar, combine rolled oats, coconut milk, vanilla protein powder, and Greek yogurt.
2. Add diced mango, raspberries, coconut flakes, chia seeds, and agave nectar if desired.
3. Mix thoroughly and refrigerate overnight.
4. Wake up to the vibrant combination of mango and raspberry!

Banana Nut Bread Protein Overnight Oats

Ingredients:
- Rolled oats (1/2 cup)
- Almond milk (1/2 cup)
- Vanilla protein powder (1 scoop)
- Banana (1, mashed)
- Walnuts (2 tbsp, chopped)
- Cinnamon (1/2 tsp)
- Nutmeg (1/4 tsp)
- Almond butter (1 tbsp)
- Maple syrup (1 tbsp, optional)

Instructions:
1. Combine rolled oats, almond milk, vanilla protein powder, and mashed banana in a jar.
2. Add chopped walnuts, cinnamon, nutmeg, almond butter, and maple syrup if desired.
3. Mix thoroughly and refrigerate overnight.
4. Enjoy the comforting taste of banana nut bread in your oats!

Chocolate Mint Protein Overnight Oats

Ingredients:
- Rolled oats (1/2 cup)
- Almond milk (1/2 cup)
- Chocolate protein powder (1 scoop)
- Greek yogurt (1/4 cup)
- Fresh mint leaves (1 tbsp, chopped)
- Dark chocolate chips (1 tbsp)
- Peppermint extract (1/4 tsp)
- Almond butter (1 tbsp)
- Agave nectar (1 tbsp, optional)

Instructions:
1. In a jar, combine rolled oats, almond milk, chocolate protein powder, and Greek yogurt.
2. Add chopped fresh mint leaves, dark chocolate chips, peppermint extract, almond butter, and agave nectar if desired.
3. Mix thoroughly and refrigerate overnight.
4. Wake up to the delightful combination of chocolate and mint in your oats!

Maple Pecan Protein Overnight Oats

Ingredients:
- Rolled oats (1/2 cup)
- Almond milk (1/2 cup)
- Vanilla protein powder (1 scoop)
- Greek yogurt (1/4 cup)
- Pecans (2 tbsp, chopped)
- Maple syrup (1 tbsp)
- Cinnamon (1/2 tsp)
- Almond butter (1 tbsp)
- Chia seeds (1 tbsp)

Instructions:
1. Combine rolled oats, almond milk, vanilla protein powder, and Greek yogurt in a jar.
2. Add chopped pecans, maple syrup, cinnamon, almond butter, and chia seeds.
3. Mix thoroughly and refrigerate overnight.
4. Enjoy the warm and cozy flavors of maple and pecan in your morning oats!

Strawberry Banana Protein Overnight Oats

Ingredients:
- Rolled oats (1/2 cup)
- Almond milk (1/2 cup)
- Vanilla protein powder (1 scoop)
- Greek yogurt (1/4 cup)
- Strawberries (1/2 cup, sliced)
- Banana (1, sliced)
- Almonds (2 tbsp, sliced)
- Honey (1 tbsp, optional)

Instructions:
1. In a jar, combine rolled oats, almond milk, vanilla protein powder, and Greek yogurt.
2. Add sliced strawberries, sliced banana, sliced almonds, and honey if desired.
3. Mix thoroughly and refrigerate overnight.
4. Wake up to the sweet and fruity combination of strawberry and banana in your oats!

Caramel Apple Protein Overnight Oats

Ingredients:
- Rolled oats (1/2 cup)
- Almond milk (1/2 cup)
- Vanilla protein powder (1 scoop)
- Greek yogurt (1/4 cup)
- Apple (1, diced)
- Caramel sauce (1 tbsp)
- Walnuts (2 tbsp, chopped)
- Cinnamon (1/2 tsp)
- Maple syrup (1 tbsp, optional)

Instructions:
1. Combine rolled oats, almond milk, vanilla protein powder, and Greek yogurt in a jar.
2. Add diced apple, caramel sauce, chopped walnuts, cinnamon, and maple syrup if desired.
3. Mix thoroughly and refrigerate overnight.
4. Enjoy the indulgent taste of caramel apple in your morning oats!

Peanut Butter & Jelly Protein Overnight Oats

Ingredients:
- Rolled oats (1/2 cup)
- Almond milk (1/2 cup)
- Vanilla protein powder (1 scoop)
- Greek yogurt (1/4 cup)
- Peanut butter (2 tbsp)
- Mixed berries (1/2 cup)
- Chia seeds (1 tbsp)
- Honey (1 tbsp, optional)

Instructions:
1. In a jar, combine rolled oats, almond milk, vanilla protein powder, and Greek yogurt.
2. Add peanut butter, mixed berries, chia seeds, and honey if desired.
3. Mix thoroughly and refrigerate overnight.
4. Wake up to the classic and beloved combination of peanut butter and jelly in your oats!

Spiced Apricot Almond Protein Overnight Oats

Ingredients:
- Rolled oats (1/2 cup)
- Almond milk (1/2 cup)
- Vanilla protein powder (1 scoop)
- Greek yogurt (1/4 cup)
- Dried apricots (2 tbsp, chopped)
- Almonds (2 tbsp, sliced)
- Ginger (1/4 tsp, ground)
- Nutmeg (1/4 tsp)
- Agave nectar (1 tbsp, optional)

Instructions:
1. Combine rolled oats, almond milk, vanilla protein powder, and Greek yogurt in a jar.
2. Add chopped dried apricots, sliced almonds, ground ginger, nutmeg, and agave nectar if desired.
3. Mix thoroughly and refrigerate overnight.
4. Enjoy the unique blend of spiced apricot and almond in your morning oats!

CONCLUSION

In conclusion, high-protein overnight oats present a versatile and nutritious breakfast option, catering to a myriad of tastes and preferences. The amalgamation of protein-rich ingredients, diverse flavors, and the convenience of preparation make these recipes an excellent choice for those seeking a wholesome start to their day.

From the refreshing fruit combinations to the indulgent dessert-inspired blends, these overnight oats provide sustained energy and promote a sense of fullness. By incorporating these recipes into your morning routine, you not only embrace a protein-packed diet but also simplify your mornings with pre-prepared, delicious meals.

Remember, adopting and adapting to this high-protein overnight oats diet is not just a culinary choice; it's a commitment to your well-being. Elevate your mornings, nourish your body, and embark on a journey towards a healthier, more energized you. Your taste buds and body will thank you for this flavorful and nutritious breakfast ritual.

BONUS: WEEKLY MEAL PLANNER JOURNAL

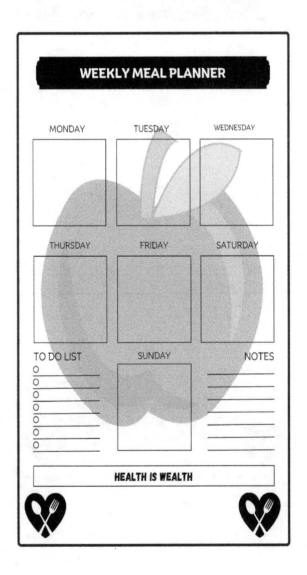

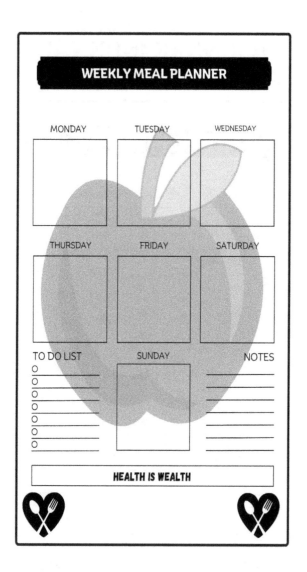

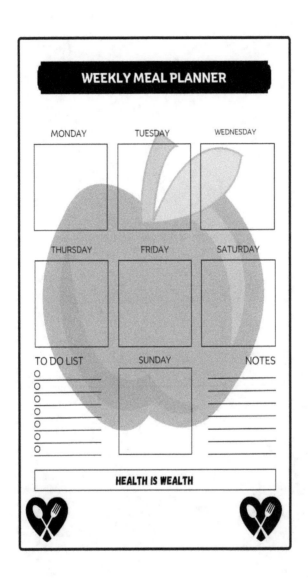

WEEKLY MEAL PLANNER

MONDAY TUESDAY WEDNESDAY

THURSDAY FRIDAY SATURDAY

TO DO LIST SUNDAY NOTES
-
-
-
-
-
-

HEALTH IS WEALTH

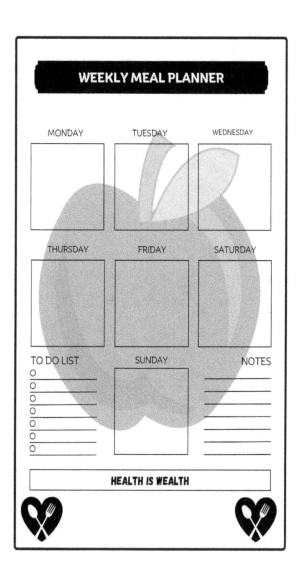

WEEKLY MEAL PLANNER

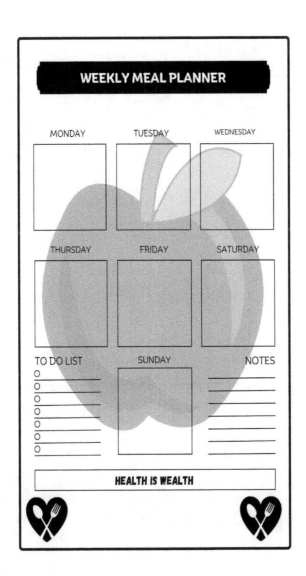

MONDAY	TUESDAY	WEDNESDAY

THURSDAY	FRIDAY	SATURDAY

TO DO LIST
- ○ _____
- ○ _____
- ○ _____
- ○ _____
- ○ _____
- ○ _____
- ○ _____

SUNDAY

NOTES
_____
_____
_____
_____
_____

HEALTH IS WEALTH

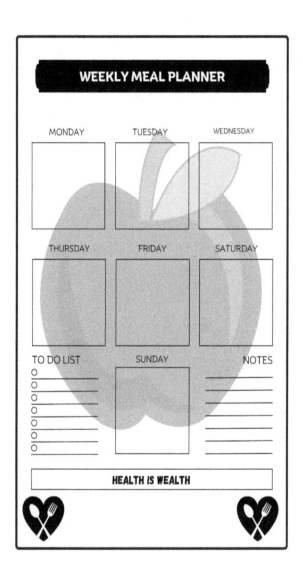

WEEKLY MEAL PLANNER

MONDAY	TUESDAY	WEDNESDAY

THURSDAY	FRIDAY	SATURDAY

TO DO LIST
-
-
-
-
-
-
-

SUNDAY

NOTES

HEALTH IS WEALTH

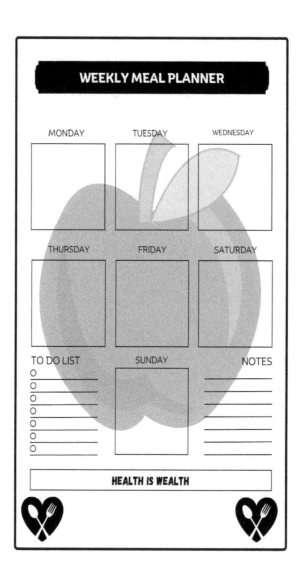

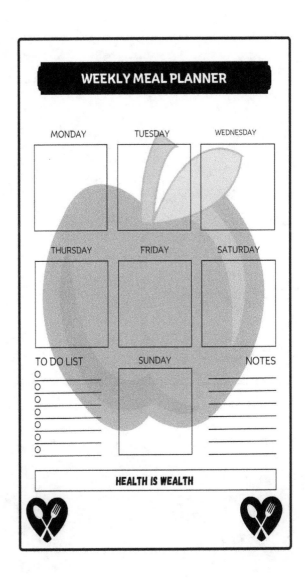

WEEKLY MEAL PLANNER

MONDAY	TUESDAY	WEDNESDAY

THURSDAY	FRIDAY	SATURDAY

TO DO LIST
-
-
-
-
-
-
-

SUNDAY

NOTES

HEALTH IS WEALTH

Printed in the USA
CPSIA information can be obtained
at www.ICGtesting.com
LVHW010417110724
785188LV00003B/252